HOOK, LINE & STINKER

First published in Great Britain in 1998 by

Chameleon Books

76 Dean Street

London W1V 5HA

Copyright for text © DC Publications Ltd

CIP data for this title is available from the British Library

ISBN 0233 99357 6

Book and jacket design by Generation Studio

Origination by Digicol Link, London

Printed in Spain by Graficas Zamudio Printek, S.A.L.

André Deutsch Ltd is a VCI plc company.

ACKNOWLEDGEMENTS:

A special thanks to all the staff, photographers and contributors to
Angling Times for their help in the compilation of this book.
Also a special thanks to Dave Crowe,
Paul Sudbury, (Veronica, Becky, Ellie & Ben) Linda Baritski, Caroline Warde,
Joanne Meekes, (and her dad), Steve, and Mark Peacock.

PHOTOGRAPH ACKNOWLEDGEMENTS

All photographs taken by Mick Rouse, chief photographer,
Angling Times.

DEDICATED TO:
Anglers Everywhere.

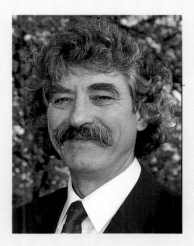

My competitive racing years and the gruelling three times a day training are now only distant memories. In those days there was never time to fish. Now a perfect day begins at dawn on the river bank, sitting peacefully, anticipating the shot of adrenalin that accompanies each twitch of the float and the sheer excitement as it dips below the water. The hunter's instincts of past generations take over and the fish is landed. On a blank day I justify my failure with the thought "fishing is not just about catching fish"...

David Bedford

BERTIE BASSETT IN
SEX TRIANGLE SHOCKER

AN EARLY START

WHOSO WILL USE the game

of angling he must rise early

which thing is profitable to man

in this wise: that is to wite, most

to the heele of his soul.

From the Treatyse on Fishing with an Angle, *1496*

7

TENCH FOR FUN

MY HUSBAND says that women can't fish! I go with him about once a month, but hadn't caught a fish all season when I joined him for a session near Wigan. On arrival I tried desperately to cast out and got my line in a right mess. I complained so much that Bill cursed and gave me his rod, while he went on the pole. Using corn on a size 14 hook with 2lb line I caught my first fish of the season, a 4lb tench, followed by a 3lb 8oz and a 3lb tench. Bill still cursed because he hadn't had a single bite. The moral of this story is, you don't have to be an expert, or a man, to enjoy the pleasures of catching a fish.

Trish Knowles

PS I do have photographs, but Bill is waiting to beat my catch before having them developed!

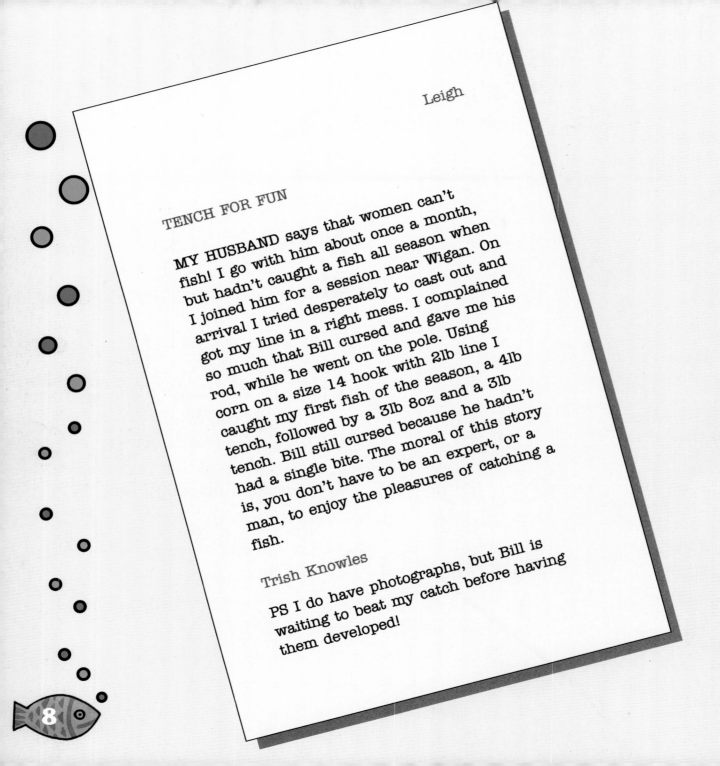

8

"NEVER SEEN ANYONE FISH A SHEEP-DIP BEFORE HAVE YOU, WOOLIE?"

FISHING THE INTERNET

FISH TALE

This fellow was fishing off the shore when he hooked a lantern. While he was drying it, all of a sudden, there was a cloud of smoke and a Genie appeared. The Genie thanked the angler for releasing him from the lantern and granted the angler three wishes. Well, the fisherman thought about it.For his 1st wish, he asked for one of each piece of fishing tackle in the BassPro Catalogue. The Genie granted his wish and there was a whole warehouse full of tackle.

For his 2nd wish, he asked for a brand new Ranger Bass Boat with all the options and a 200hp Mercury Outboard. His 2nd wish was granted and there was a fully rigged Ranger Bass Boat and a 200hp Merc.

Now, he really had to think about his last wish. He asked that he be able to live a long, long life and be able to fish every minute of everyday.

The Genie granted his final wish. The fisherman turned into a GREAT BLUE HERON.

FISHING RULE #1
The least experienced fisherman always catches the biggest fish...

"BLOODY 'ELL, I'VE SNEEZED MY BRAIN OUT!"

"SO HAVE I!"

FISH OUT OF WATER

Jim had an awful day fishing, sitting in the blazing sun all day without catching a single one.

On his way home, he stopped at the supermarket and ordered two trout. He told the fish salesman, *Pick two large ones out and throw them at me, will you?*

Why do you want me to throw them at you? the salesman replied.

Because I want to tell my wife that I caught them! said Jim.

Oh, now I understand, but you better take this salmon instead.

Why? replied Jim.

Because your wife came in earlier today and said that when you come by, I should tell you she would prefer salmon for supper tonight.

13

"IT'S...UH...UH...
A PLASTIC THING. I THINK."

DOUBLE WHAMMY

There is a pool in Norway's famous Alta river called Sierra. The neck of the pool is 75 yards long with fast-flowing, deep water under the right bank, while on the left bank there is a deep back-eddy. The angler is canoed over the eddy to fish the fast water and if he hooks a fish is rowed back and put ashore. A Norwegian angler played a fish in this backwater and simply could not bring it in. As the salmon, when hooked, had not seemed inordinately large for the Alta, the puzzled gillie looked into the deep water and saw a huge fish in some kind of distress. He gaffed it and pulled out a 51-pounder with the angler's fly-line lassoed round its tail. He released the line and the rod then landed the 26-pounder which had taken his fly.

Billee Chapman Pincher, Fish Tales, *1989*

FISHING RULE #2
The worse your line is tangled, the better is the fishing around you...

RASH MOVE

An athletic fisherman with a painful tale is Vane Ivanovic, who represented his native Yugoslavia in the 1936 Berlin Olympics (in water polo and hurdling). One day, while diving off Formentora in Majorca, he speared a 1lb blackfish and decided to carry it back to shore stuffed down the front of his swimming trunks. A few weeks later he developed a skin rash in an embarrassing area and was sent to see a specialist who, with considerable professional excitement, told him he was the first human to be found suffering from a form of ringworm peculiar to fishes. "It is my duty to report this event in *The Lancet*," the specialist explained. "May I have your permission to use your name for the benefit of other doctors and their patients?" It is not known whether Ivanovic accepted this dubious medical honour.

Billee Chapman Pincher, Fish Tales, *1989*

"LOOK WHAT I CAUGHT IN MY PINT."

A DOG'S LIFE

PEOPLE WHO claim to own "fishing dogs" are all blinded by love. There's no such thing as a good fishing dog. Most of these beasts are retrievers who think they can do to trout what they've been trained to do to ducks. It may sound cute, but it's not. Stay away from people who take their dogs fishing.

John Gierach, Trout Bum, *1986*

YOU'VE BEEN WARNED

THE LATE fishing guru Hugh Falkus, co-author of *Freshwater Fishing,* was celebrated for many things, including surviving four years as a POW after his Spitfire was shot down in the war. He also had a tendency to be outspoken about some of his fellow anglers – "there's no one sillier than an educated person with no commonsense" – and he was fond of strong language. In the days when he had fishing on the River Esk, signs to deter poachers mentioned nothing so tame as privacy – they simply read "F**k Off!".

DANGERS OF FISHING

AMONG THE OBVIOUS dangers of fishing there is, firstly, the risk from the water itself. Every year, Farlow's, the fishing tackle shop in Pall Mall, loses a couple of customers who have slipped while wading a river and drowned. At least, that's what the manager claimed last year. I recall that he was trying to sell me a pair of inflatable braces at the time.

Jeremy Paxman, Fish, Fishing and the Meaning of Life, *1994*

ANGRY MONSTER

At CRONULLA, New South Wales, in March 1934, two fishermen caught a 12-foot shark on a line about six miles off the coast. The enraged monster immediately speared into an attack on the solid 18-foot launch. Several times it drove its great weight at the launch, snapping viciously at the rudder and bow, causing the boat to rock violently. The two men were mightily relieved to be taken aboard a larger launch. Meanwhile, the shark continued its attack on the smaller boat. The shark fought every inch of the way for an hour before it was landed. Several mako shark's teeth were later extracted from the launch's timber.

V M Coppleson, Shark Attack, *1958*

"I once gave up FISHING, it was the most terrifying weekend of my life".

LIVING DANGEROUSLY

IN SHORT, if a 12-foot tiger shark grows fond of you and moves in for a closer acquaintance, do what you can to repel it, but don't be too optimistic about the outcome, for the shark is in its element and is considerably stronger and more durable than a human being. Your brain is almost four times as large as its, though, and if properly applied, may help prolong the struggle until help arrives or you win through to safety.

David Webster, Myth and Maneater, *1962*

"RIGHT," HE SAID, "JUST HOLD THE ROD - THIS FISHING GAME IS EASY!"

FISHERMAN'S FRIENDS

Fishing is the 2nd greatest thrill known to man, CATCHING is the first.

A BIT OF THE OTHER

HELEN ARCHER knows exactly how to get her hubby Tim in the mood for a night of passion – all it takes is a big fish! So the fantastic 6lb 1oz black bream that Helen caught on her first-ever fishing trip was bound to set the sheets alight. She explained, "It's a bit of a joke between me and my husband. In the past we have always celebrated Tim's big catches with a bit of the other, but this time I thought I might be in for a double helping!" Tim was delighted with Helen's catch, saying: "It was straight upstairs for a night of passion, and I hope the tradition continues!" Helen said: "I hear the lads are now planning a shark fishing trip… "

SEX ON THE MENU

SCIENTISTS are so confident that women's "sex signals" make them irresistible to fish they've made it a bait flavouring! The mystery over female pheromones has raged for years with tales of trout anglers using their wives' pubic hair to dress flies. And a new company claims it has reproduced pheromones to create the ultimate bait-flavouring spray. But one woman who says you can't beat the real thing is London angler Jane N'Dure. Halfway through her third season, Jane has already won three match trophies. She said: "Trouble was, quite a few of the lads suggested ways of sharing my pheromones… need I say more?"

23

THE MARRIED ANGLER'S TEN COMMANDMENTS

(According to Chris Thornhill, Chatham, Kent)

1. Thou shalt not use the wife's blender. Thou shalt buy one's own.
2. Thou shalt not sneak maggots into the fridge when wife has gone to bed.
3. Thou shalt clean up the kitchen after a "bait making explosion".
4. Thou shalt not use the "but the fish started biting" excuse when one is late.
5. Thou shalt not try to explain the fascination of fishing.
6. Thou shalt not nick all the sweetcorn and dog biscuits.
7. Thou shalt tell her that 10kg of boilies cost just five quid.
8. Thou shalt not keep a saw within a two-mile radius of one's rods.
9. Thou shalt not sneak a telescopic rod in one's suitcase for the family holiday in Spain.
10. Thou shalt hide away one's *Angling Times* before one's wife feeds them all to the bin man.

PIKE TROUBLE AND STRIFE

WAR HAS BEEN declared between an angling-mad couple over who caught their biggest ever pike. Christine and Martin Gott were at loggerheads on their local canal when he landed the predator while it was attached to her tackle. Fellow anglers looked on in amazement as the feuding couple then argued which Gott got the pike. Mother-of-two Christine had tempted the 9lb pike on the Leeds-Liverpool Canal at Bingley, West Yorkshire, with two maggots intended for gudgeon. But when the predator snapped her flimsy 2lb line, the drama seemed over... until Bradford engineer Martin, 49, hooked his wife's float and discovered the pike still attached! He eased the pike to the bank after a ten minute fight. "We're still arguing about it," joked Christine, 50, an administrator for a security firm. "It was caught on my gear so I'm definitely claiming it."

24

"BIRDS OF A FEATHER"

SWAN VISTA

SPROUT FEVER

MADCAP CARP MAN Rick Cornforth has launched an all-out assault to catch a British record carp – on a Brussels sprout! Rick is spurning hi-tech boilies in his conviction that vegetarian grass carp at £5-a-day Bluebell Lakes in Northants will appreciate a hair-rigged, popped-up sprout. Rick, who recently lost a huge grass carp at the venue – which he believes would have smashed the 28lb 12oz record – said: "The carp should appreciate the chance to eat something other than weed."

BEANZ MEANZ CARP

MATCH ANGLER Garry Goodson blew away the opposition with a 39p tin of Heinz baked beans. The canny angler turned to the high-protein snack when conventional baits failed. And the wind of change followed as Garry, of Kettering, Northants, blitzed the fishery record with a stunning 72lb carp haul.

Two Irishmen went fishing.
They caught a lot of fish and returned to the shore.
1st Irishman said I hope you remember the spot where we caught all those fish
2nd Irishman said Yes, I made an 'X' on the side of the boat to mark the spot.
1st Irishman said You idiot! How do you know that we'll get the same boat?

Wallasey, Cheshire

I'M HUMAN TOO!

I WOULD LIKE to ask male anglers why they ignore me. I fish once a week with my boyfriend, we always fish neighbouring swims, and I have lost count of the number of times an angler has spoken to my boyfriend yet ignored me. I don't bite!

Val Haley

PHILOSOFISHY

If you wish to be happy for one hour, get intoxicated.
If you wish to be happy for three days, get married.
If you wish to be happy for eight days, kill your pig and eat it.
If you wish to be happy forever....learn to fish!

TOO EASY

Take a gudgeon, and stick the hook either through his upper lip, or back fin, and throw him into the likely haunts before mentioned, swimming at mid-water. When the pike takes it, let him run a little, as at the snap, and then strike him. In this method of pike fishing, you may take three kinds of fish, viz. pikes, pearch and chubs. It is so murdering a way that the generous angler should never use it, except he wants a few fish to present his friends with.

Thomas Best, A Concise Treatise on the Art of Angling, *1787*

BUNNY OLD GAME

FORGET MORE EXOTIC baits and flavourings – carp are going ga-ga for rabbit droppings! It's now thought that tiny pellets of bunny poo could be the most radical carp bait since Dick Walker par-boiled a potato. Caldicot angler Dave Williams stumbled on the revolutionary bait after he heard about anglers using pigeon droppings in their groundbait. Dave, 50, explained: "I was having a right laugh about Van den Eynde pigeon s**t groundbait in my tackle shop. But I tried mixing some rabbit droppings in with my maggots on my next trip and they really worked, accounting for several carp in the 5lb range."

STRIKING A SALMON

I UNHESITATINGLY assert that there is no single moment with horse or gun into which is concentrated such a thrill of hope, fear, expectation and exultation as that of the rise and successful striking of a heavy salmon. I have seen men literally unable to stand, or to hold their rod, from sheer excitement. And indeed in this very excitement - in the impetuosity of spirit it engenders - lies almost the only real difficulty of salmon fishing.

H Cholmondeley Pennell,
The Modern Practical Angler, *1870*

SWEET SUCCESS

SUPERMARKET SHELVES and sweet shops across the country are being mercilessly raided as anglers everywhere search for strange bag-up baits. In recent seasons scores of fish have been taken on jelly, Liquorice Allsorts, strawberrys, jam and sprouts. But there can only be one winner and the decision was a tough one – Wine Gums and Liquorice Allsorts have come out neck and neck in most trials – but the Wacky Bait World Cup Champions remain, Allsorts.

29

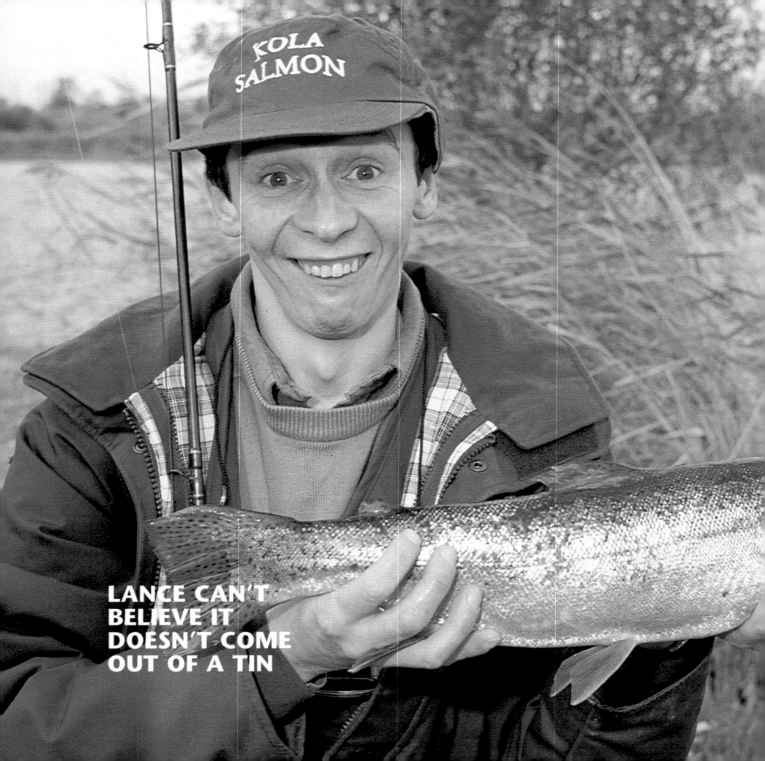

LANCE CAN'T
BELIEVE IT
DOESN'T COME
OUT OF A TIN

FISHERMAN'S FRIENDS

A jerk at one end of the line waiting for a jerk at the other end of the line.

HOPPING MAD

FRANKENSTEIN FISH could be hopping our way after madcap scientists crossed a salmon with a rabbit. Known as 'Babe', the creature has been artificially engineered to produce a type of fish protein in its milk which can be used as a medicinal aid for human bone conditions. Dr Heather Hall of London Zoo says: "Scientists have been carrying out lots of useful genetic manipulation with fish for some time. Salmon have been bred with anti-freeze in their blood to stop them freezing solid in cold water. And fish farmers already breed single-sex super fish."

31

WHAT THE BEST DRESSED ANGLERS ARE WEARING TODAY

HE'S CAUGHT
TWO FISH TODAY

THE THREE MEN AND A FART TEAM CATCH

CANINE CARPER

A DOG caught a 3lb mirror carp after an angler left his peg for a call of nature. Mark Newton had vacated the swim for only a minute when he returned to see the mirror motoring off into the horizon still attached to his pole! But after Mark "nearly drowned" trying to save his tackle, Monster, his neighbour's Irish wolfhound cross, leaped into action. The dog jumped into the lake, grabbed the 12-foot telescopic pole and dragged it to the bank at Gwinear Fishery, Cornwall. When he retrieved his gear, Mark, 22, found that Monster had managed to successfully play the still-hooked fish to complete one of the year's most unusual catches.

HATS OFF TO JAMES

A HARD HAT and caster was the weird cocktail James Parkin used to win an epic battle with a 16lb carp. Fishing his local Hopton Waters, the "Dewsbury Daredevil" donned a protective helmet to brave a bombardment of golf balls from the adjacent driving range in his quest for a big fish. James, 24, explained: "I decided to fish on the bank near the golf driving range and the bailiff told me to wear a hard hat. While I played the fish, golf balls were flying everywhere – one of them hit my seat box and others landed in the water." After a manic half-hour battle, James netted his prize.

FISHERMAN'S FRIENDS

Nothing grows faster than a fish from the time that it bites until the time that it gets away!!

37

AN ODE BY BOBBY GEORGE

'An Ode by BOBBY GEORGE

Please do not write any wit
upon these walls because you
would think Shakespear had been
here to write them all.

Because fingers arn't brushes
and shit isn't paint.

And if you think it's funny well
it fucking well ain't!!!

Bobby George

ICE RELIEF

ICEBERGS could be the answer to Britain's drought-hit rivers. In a desperate bid, water bosses have hatched madcap plans to float icebergs from the Arctic. The zany scheme is being considered by Essex and Suffolk Water following a nightmare 75 per cent drop in normal water resource levels to supply over one million water users.

ALL STUCK UP

MATCHMAN Ben McGrath isn't shouting about his latest victory… after super-gluing his mouth shut! Things got a little sticky when Ben tried to glue dog biscuits to his hook during a match near Guildford. "It was a nightmare! I was trying to take the lid off the tube when it split open at the side and filled my mouth with glue. Luckily I managed to prize open my lips and carry on fishing." Ben, from Horsham, West Sussex, also managed to glue his hand to his pole. Amazingly, he went on to win the match, taking 20 carp for 60lb.

OL' GLUE EYES

AMERICAN FISHERY BOFFINS have unveiled a crazy plan to give fish glass eyes. Scientists Dr Greg Lewbart and Robert Bakal have developed the £300 operation to replace the damaged eyes of koi carp. Keeping the Japanese ornamental fish is a multi-million dollar industry in America, and fussy owners are prepared to splash out to keep their prize specimens looking perfect.

NO PLAICE TO GO

A TURBO-CHARGED PLAICE swam more than 600 miles in just two months to find a mate – only to end up served up with a plate of chips! The fantastic flattie's journey was tracked by Government scientists using a satellite after it was fitted with a micro-tag and released off the Norfolk coast. The love-sick flattie first zoomed up to Yorkshire's Flamborough Head in an unsuccessful bid to find a partner. Undeterred, he swam back down to the English Channel spawning grounds off Brighton – then headed back to Norfolk. But the move proved fatal as the lonely plaice was caught by a passing trawler, and sold to a fish and chip shop!

39

HOOKED AGAIN

While fishing the River Lea in Hertfordshire with a Gold-ribbed Hare's Ear on a 3lb tippet, I hooked from the bank a sizeable rainbow trout. After a couple of seconds I parted company with the fish and inspection of the tackle revealed that some 18 inches of the leader, plus the nymph, were missing. An unnoticed wind knot must have been to blame. Replacing the leader and nymph, this time with a Pheasant-tail, I saw a rise near the same weed bed where I had just lost my fish. A cast over this spot hooked a rainbow, which I safely netted. It crossed my mind that this might be the same fish that I had lost, and after unhooking the Pheasant-tail, I duly found the GRHE hooked into the roof of its mouth, with the length of tippet curled round the fly like a coil of rope round a quayside bollard.

Harold Buckley,
Trout & Salmon, October 1990

SCOTCH SWORDFISH

A HUGE SWORDFISH was found in a Scottish loch – after making an epic 1,800-mile trip from the warm waters off Spain. The 250lb broadbill was discovered washed up on the bonny banks of Loch Long by shocked boat hire boss Tony Hebson. It had swum nearly 50 miles inland up the famed loch, some 20 miles west of Glasgow. Stunned Tony, who found the beast floating just 100 yards off the loch shore, said: "When I first spotted it I thought it was a dead seal. Then I boated out to it and saw its huge bill – it was incredible."

PHILOSOFISHY
There's a fine line between fishing and just sitting on the bank looking like an idiot.

GENDER BENDERS

SEX-CHANGE FISH in Britain's rivers are caused by oestrogen from women's urine, claims a new report. Scientists at Brunel University and the Ministry of Agriculture, Fisheries and Food have pinpointed the human female hormone oestrogen as the reason why some fish have been found to have both male and female traits. Oestrogen enters rivers via sewage treatment works. Male roach subjected to oestrogenic laced effluent suffered a lower spawning potential.

TO BOLDLY SWIM

FOUR FISH have boldly gone where they have never been before – into space! The fish-stronaughtical quartet was blasted into orbit on the space shuttle Columbia. The shooting stars also became the first organisms to fornicate at the final frontier when two of them produced 15 fry – the first space babes. The idea behind the launch was to see if the Medaka, a 5cm long silvery South East Asian cyprinid, could eventually be used to feed men on the moon.

IT'S GOT TO BE GORDON

JINXED GORDON BUTLER didn't think his day could get much worse when his seatbox collapsed. But despite a sore backside the 70-year-old soldiered on, only to find a fish had powered off with his rod and reel while his back was turned at Pryor Farm, South Nutfield, Surrey. Gordon fished on only to be tripped up by the angler on the next peg. He came crashing down on his landing net, smashing the handle and collecting a few more bumps on his now weary body. Gordon, of Epsom, said "My mate was laughing for days afterwards. My pride was a little hurt but I'm still fishing."

SERIOUS SQUID

A NEW scientific expedition plans to lower a camera deep into waters off New Zealand in a bid to capture the first 60 foot giant squid on film. Dr Clyde Roper of the Smithsonian National Museum of Natural History, in Washington, USA said: "It's staggering that this big animal exists and we know hardly anything about it. In fact, we know more about dinosaurs."

41

"AFTER A HARD DAY'S FISHING ME AND THE MAGGOTS LIKE TO HAVE A RELAXING DRINK."

BOFFINS ON NET

FISHERY CHIEFS have moved into Cyberspace! The Environment Agency has launched an internet website, featuring information about key river flows, selected river habitats and water quality. Visitors to the site can zoom in on their local area using maps or postcode-based searches and can easily download information on to their own computers. The site address is: www.environment-agency.gov.uk.

FISH & QUIPS

Q. What did the fish say when he swam into a wall?

A. Damn!

WHAT'S EATING YOU?

MANY BELIEVE angling is great therapy - but Michael Short literally owes his health to a trip to Turkey where he claims being eaten alive by carp has cured his painful skin disease. Michael, 23, suffers from Psoriasis, and received fin-tastic treatment by lying in a pool with a species of tiny carp - known as the Little Doctor Fish of Kangal. Michael, from Belfast, explained how they nibbled through his skin: "They put me through hell but my skin is now back to normal and I'm incredibly grateful."

43

SEAMAN'S OWN GOAL

ENGLAND GOALIE David Seaman has won an award for not being able to catch. The Arsenal star missed out while everyone else was sacking up with trout at Hanningfield's annual Pro-Am day, prompting staff at the Essex stillwater to award him the booby prize.

EMLYN NETS ANOTHER

SOCCER LEGEND Emlyn Hughes had never managed a trout bigger than 2lb 8oz when he hooked a giant on his first-ever visit to Ladybower Reservoir. The former Liverpool and England captain was delighted to boat a cracking grown-on 7lb 3oz rainbow at the top Derbyshire water. 'Crazy Horse' Emlyn, 49, admitted, "As soon as I hit it I knew it was a big one, but I had no idea just how big."

OWZAT! I'D HATE TO SEE THE BIRD THAT LET GO OF THIS!

Q. HOW DO YOU KISS
A PIKE?
A. VERY CAREFULLY.

CHAMPION HAUL

PAUL INGLE, the British Featherweight champion, swapped punches for slabs in a night fishing session at Scarborough Mere. The gloves came off as the 25 year old local lad banked 40lb of bream on only his second fishing trip. Paul, whose ring name is 'Naz Hunter' is managed by Lennox Lewis's boss Frank Maloney. "Fishing helps me wind down," he says. "It is really relaxing."

TARRANT TELLS ALL

ZANY TV STAR Chris Tarrant has revealed his testicles once turned black when they were electrocuted on a fishing trip to the River Kennet in Berkshire. The accident-prone DJ frazzled his most delicate parts when he urinated against an electric fence. Keen angler Chris, said, "There is no pain on earth like being electrocuted straight up the tinkle box. I screamed and lay there quivering, still unzipped, for several minutes."

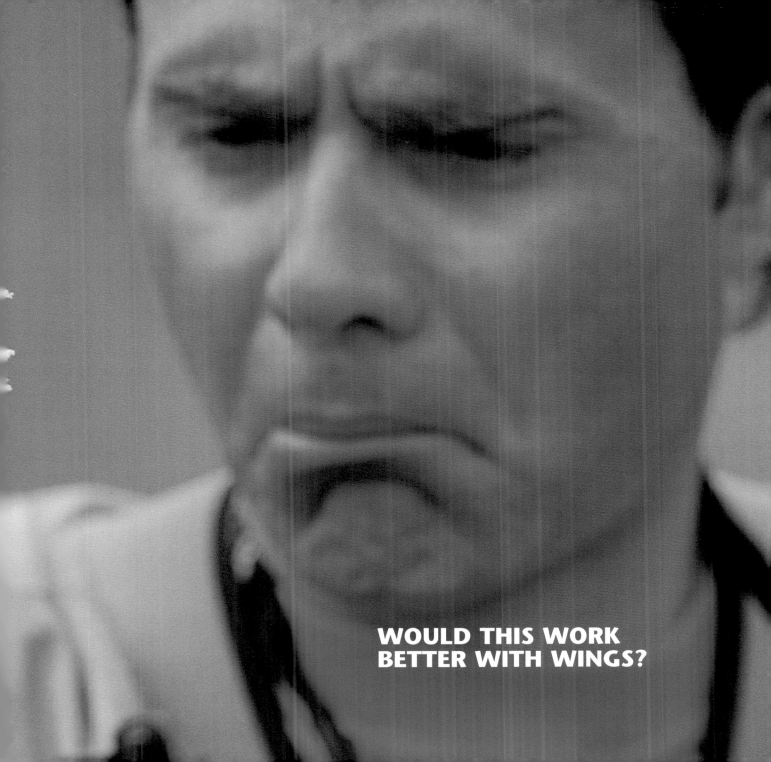

WOULD THIS WORK
BETTER WITH WINGS?

ESSEX GIRLS DO IT
SITTING DOWN

**IT'S NOT ABOUT SIZE...
IT'S WHAT YOU DO
WITH IT THAT COUNTS**

GOODBYE GIRLS!

A FISHING match was ruined when a boat load of drunken college girls pestered anglers for sex. Matchmen raised their poles when they saw the scantily-clad students approach on the Oxford Canal. But instead of sailing quietly by, the boozy Hooray Henriettas rammed the barge into the bank, teased anglers about the size of their tackle and demanded sex. But while they turned the air blue, hard-nosed matchmen saw red as the girls' saucy antics turned the fish off. Shocked match organiser Pat O'Connor said: "I've never seen anything like it. The girls were dancing on the top of the boat with music blasting out. They were totally out of control."

53

ANGLERS... WHAT A
CRAZY BUNCH OF
MIXED UP KIDS

"FINALLY A PAPER THAT DOESN'T MENTION THE WORLD CUP."

GAZZA INJURY SCARE

ENGLAND FOOTBALLER and keen angler Paul Gascoigne came within inches of serious injury after an argument with a press photographer at a Berkshire trout fishery. During the row the Daily Mirror photographer drove his car through a locked five-bar farm gate at the fishery, and straight across a main road. The incident happened after Gazza demanded the photographer's film and fishery owner Ron Dane shut and chained the entrance gate. Gazza, along with fellow England players David Seaman and Ian Walker, was relaxing at Sheep House Farm fishery near Maidenhead, Berkshire.

FISH & QUIPS

Don't go swimming, a shark just bit off my foot!
Which one?
I don't know. All sharks look the same to me.

CUBAN JAWS ENCOUNTER

A HUNGRY SHARK grabbed a sea angler's catch, then decided it wanted a piece of his rod as well! Charter boat boss Roger Bayzand was fly fishing in Cuba when the big predator struck. "I was playing a bonefish when this grey shape appeared," said Roger. He jumped out of the water and reeled in the fish until it was just nine feet away – then the six-foot reef shark pounced. "It grabbed the fish then I thrashed the water with the end of my rod to try and frighten it off," said Roger, from Lymington, Hants. "But it just bit the end off!"

A FISH OUT OF WATER

GORD BURTON, PIKE ANGLER
V
BARRY McGUIGAN, BOXER

I'LL STICK TO THE FISHING THANKS BAZ

FISHERMAN'S FRIENDS

One man's hobby was fishing, he spent all his weekends fishing, paying no attention to the weather.

One Sunday, early in the morning, he went to the river. It was cold and raining, and the fish weren't biting, so he decided to return back to his house.

He came in, went to his bedroom, undressed and laid next to his wife.

"What terrible weather today, honey", he said to her.

"Yes. And my idiot husband went fishing!"

59

MICE AND TROUT

I HAVE NEVER seen a rainbow trout take a vole, but a 2lb rainbow I caught on the River Test at Leckford this summer had a vole stuck in its gullet, partly digested. I have also twice caught fish with field-mice in their stomachs, one in a fish of about 2lb, also at Leckford, and the other in a 1lb 4oz rainbow caught in a lake at Petworth Park.

Mrs K Liverman,
Trout & Salmon, December 1989

CARP MAN DONE GOOD

ROB HALES, one of Britain's top carp fishermen, is the man behind the Golden Bear toy company responsible for the teletubbies mania which recently swept the country. Rob is boss of the firm which won the contract to produce the toys based on the BBC television hit.

FISH & QUIPS

What do you call a fish with no eye?

FSH!!!!

THREE-MINUTE TRIUMPH

A ONE-ARMED ANGLER took on one of Cheshire's biggest carp... and won! Stoke-On-Trent specimen hunter Simon Mugglestone landed the 32 lb 3 oz mirror during a session on a local stillwater and, despite being born without a left arm below the elbow, netted the fish inside three minutes. Simon said: "I've got an artificial forearm which is brilliant and there was no problem playing and landing the fish, despite it's size."

DENIAL IS NOT ONLY A RIVER IN EGYPT

INT FISHING BRILLIANT

PURPLE DACE

THAT'S THE PLAQUE REMOVED AND NOW FOR THE FILLING!

BALTIC PIKE BONANZA

A HUNT for giant predators produced the world's best-ever haul of pike. Swedish angler Dick Persson landed a massive 44lb pike, followed by two others of 37lb 8oz and 35lb – and all in the same session!

The incredible catch was made at a secret location on Sweden's Baltic coast, and was witnessed by well known English specimen hunters Mick Brown and Graham Marsden. Graham said: "We both realised that this could be the biggest pike triple ever taken by a single angler."

IRISH EYES ARE SMILING

IN 1989 SEAMUS BARRETT and his son caught 46 grilse between them in one day from the Ridge Pool of the River Moy in Ireland. Following publication of a photograph of the happy fishers and their catch in the angling press, reactions ranged from "Well done, Mr Barrett – a splendid angling achievement! This will be a photograph to treasure, a record to show your grandchildren..." to accusations of "butchery", "slaughter" and "bloodlust".

WILLSON'S NEW PLUMMETTING METHOD NEEDS REVISTING

SHOCK ESCAPE

TEENAGER Anthony Mellor survived 11,000 volts – thanks to his trusty pair of waders. The 15-year-old diced with death when his carbon pole touched overhead cables at a tiny pond. But while his pole was frazzled, Anthony escaped with a few tiny burn marks to his hand due to his rubber soles acting as electricity insulators. The shaken angler said: "There was a great crack and the pole shook in my hand. I dropped it straight away." A police officer who was at the scene said: "Anthony was very lucky. We gave him first aid until the ambulance arrived."

65

FISH TALE

Three fishermen were fishing when they came upon a mermaid, who offered them one wish each. So the first fisherman said, "DOUBLE MY I.Q," and the mermaid did it. To his surprise he started reciting Shakespeare plays perfectly.

Then the second fisherman said, "TRIPLE MY I.Q", and sure enough the mermaid did it. Amazingly, the fisherman started doing mathematical problems he didn't know existed.

The third fisherman was so impressed, he asked the mermaid, "QUADRUPLE MY I.Q"! The mermaid warned the fisherman, are you sure about this? It will change your whole life! The fisherman replied "of course I am sure".

So the mermaid turned him into a woman.

FISH & QUIPS

How do you stop a fish from smelling?

Cut its nose off.

AMERICAN ICE FISHING

A guy was fishing through a hole in the ice, and after half-an-hour was getting nowhere. He thought that maybe the fish were clumping in some other areas, so he decided to drill another hole. After another wasted half-an-hour, he started drilling yet another hole when he heard a voice saying, "THERE ARE NO FISH UNDER THE ICE". The bemused fellow paused for a moment, and carried on. Again came the voice, "THERE ARE NO FISH UNDER THE ICE"!

The guy somewhat awed, said "Is that you, God"?

And the voice replied "NO, IT'S THE MANAGER OF THE ICE RINK"!

66

"DAMM THOSE FLYING FISH - I'LL SHOW THEM"

A DUEL TO
THE DEATH
OVER THE
SIZE OF A
FISH

TENCH AND PIKE

The Tench is the physician of fishes, for the Pike especially, and that the Pike, being either sick or hurt, is cured by the touch of the Tench. And it is observed that the tyrant Pike will not be wolf to his physician, but forbears to devour him though he be never so hungry.

Izaak Walton, The Compleat Angler, *1676*

HEAD OF A GIANT

THE HUGE pike skull which was discovered at the mouth of the River Endrick in 1934 is believed to have belonged to the biggest pike in history. No less an expert than Dick Walker estimated the predator weighed 70lb – 24lb more than the current British record – based on the head's enormous proportions.

FISH & QUIPS

If fish lived on land, which country would they live in?

Finland.

WD40 BEST FOR PIKE

PIKE ANGLER John Devonshire showed bream-bashing match anglers how to do it as he won a competition using baits covered in WD40 lubricant! John, from Langley, Slough, had travelled to Ireland's Lough Ree for a pike session but decided to enter the match and try his luck alongside the swimfeeder and pole brigade. The other matchmen laughed when he covered his roach deadbait with his "secret weapon", WD40, but they saw him land pike of 27lb, 21lb and 18lb to win. "I've had a 35lb pike on WD40," said John. "The smell of it brings them on."

FISHING IS A GAME OF SKILL, FINESSE,
JUDGEMENT, TECHNIQUE, A KEEN EYE...
OR JUST PURE BLIND LUCK.

OOH SORRY!!!

ROACHES

£7 AN INCH

ONE-AND-A-HALF miles of one of the world's top salmon rivers went up for sale at a mind-blowing £7 an inch! The Aberdeenshire Dee between Durris and Culter, famous for huge salmon, was for sale at £585,000, or a cool £7 per inch of bank. A spokesman for estate agents Savills said: "The rarity of a beat of this quality coming on to the market will attract keen interest."

WHAT HAPPENED?

AMERICAN ANGLER

An obsessed individual who owns a house that is falling down due to neglect, a truck whose colour can best be described as Rust-Oleum, and a pristine bass boat that he chamois' down methodically before and after each trip.

73

GREG RUSEDSKI
DOESN'T HAVE THIS
TROUBLE WITH
HEADBANDS

LUKKI FIND

PIKE FISHERMAN Harry Milligan was in a spin during a trip to his local reservoir after landing a net full of glittering jewels. The Manchester predator hunter was busy trying out a new pike rod on Rhodes Reservoir when his aptly named 'Lukki' spinner hooked into a sports bag full of sunken treasure. Included was a huge haul of Rolex watches, gold jewellery, an inscribed clock dated back to the 1800's and a platinum brooch encrusted with precious stones. 'Lukki Harry' handed the haul to his local police station for safe-keeping and, if no-one claims it within a few weeks, it will be his. But amazingly Harry says: "I've found my treasure but I'd much prefer to see it returned to the rightful owners."

FISH & QUIPS

What has big sharp teeth, a tail, scales, and a trunk?

A pike going on holiday.

FISH & QUIPS

Where do you find a crab with no legs?
Exactly where you left it.

THUMB

A temporary hook holder.

FISH & QUIPS

Man: Can I have a fly rod and reel for my son?
Fishing Shop Owner: Sorry sir we don't do swaps.

Sutton-in-Ashfield, Notts

CURSE OF ANGLING

I FISH OPEN matches every month on our local water. Yes, men do swear but so do women! I know I have done my share of cursing, especially when I lose a big fish or when people walk past and say, 'I didn't think a woman would have the patience to fish.' As for when you happen to see men answering the call of nature, just say in a loud voice: 'It's a good job you're fishing on maggot, mate, because that wouldn't catch a thing!' Maybe next time he'll be a bit more cautious about where he 'waters his horse'.

M. Townsend

DUE TO THE POSSIBILITY
OF MISS-HIT GOLF BALLS,
THIS PEG TO BE USED
AT OWN RISK.

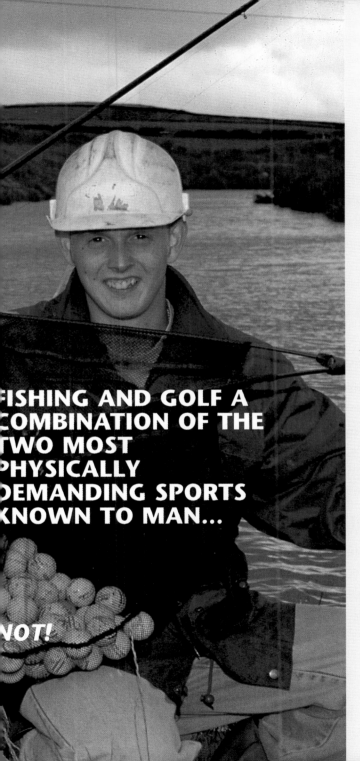

FISHING AND GOLF A COMBINATION OF THE TWO MOST PHYSICALLY DEMANDING SPORTS KNOWN TO MAN...

NOT!

HALLS AND HIS BALLS

CARP ANGLERS are proclaiming the benefits of big balls – of bait, that is – for carp. Martyn Halls used 24mm boilies to catch a cracking 49lb 12oz mirror from an ultra-tough Kent water. So what is it about "gobstoppers" which gives them that vital edge? There are five main advantages, believes Martyn:

1. They are different to standard baits, and thus less suspicious-looking to wary fish.
2. Bigger baits mean more flavour leaks out and provide the fish with a more attractive food target.
3. A highly visible bait can be a big advantage if fish are feeding hard, or if bottom silt and weed obscures standard baits.
4. They can be fed accurately and at very long range, even if there is a strong wind blowing.
5. Heavyweight baits act as a superb anti-tangle device.

79

RECOVERY JOB

A QUICK PINT helped John Senior to a surprise catch other anglers couldn't reach – and landed him a free night on the beer. The 51-year-old returned to his swim and, amazingly, hooked into the cork butt of the rod his fishing partner Trev had lost earlier that day. He managed to land both rod and reel while Trev shouted, "If tha' gets it out, John, tha's drinking for nowt tonight." John, who finally eased the gear ashore, said, "All Trev's line had gone and so had the suspected barbel, but he was just happy to get his rod and reel back."

AGE-OLD COMPLAINT

Fishing, if I a fisher may protest,

Of pleasures is the sweetest, of sports the best,

Of exercises the most excellent,

Of recreations the most innocent.

But now the sport is marde, and wott ye why?

Fishes decrease, and fishers multiply.

Thomas Bastard, Chrestoleros, *1598 1870*

MIRACLE FROM THE DEPTHS AMAZED ANGLER

BILL MCMILLAN landed a catch in a million – the fishing rod he lost in a lake years ago. He hooked the rare £150 rod on a recent return to the 100-acre Loch Kindar, near New Abbey. Bill, who runs a tackle shop in Dumfries, said: "For me to see it again is unbelievable. The fly went right through a rod ring and it came up like the Mary Rose." Bill, 67, lost the rod in July 1993, when it fell overboard from his boat as he sped to shore to escape a storm.

80

TO ANGLERS
THIS IS A BIRD
OF PREY

PIG TALES

FISH TALES

SWAMP HERO ALF

MOVE OVER Crocodile Dundee, Britain now has its own all-action swamp hero – Alligator Alf! Sixty-four-year-old angler Alf Hilton became an unlikely star when he fought a hungry reptile on holiday in Florida. But unlike Mick Dundee in the hit film, the retired painter and decorator didn't beat the ferocious snapper with his bare hands – he simply used a Frankfurter sausage. That was the tasty treat Alf had served up to tempt giant catfish on Gospel Island. When the hungry beast snaffled his sausage, the iron-willed Mancunian calmly played out and beached the alligator on a telescopic rod and 5lb line. "I wasn't frightened at all," said Alligator Alf. "It was beautiful to feel, a bit like a snake. Catching it made my day."

FISH & QUIPS

What is yellow and dangerous?
Pike infested custard.

FISHING RULE #3

Fishing will do a lot for a man but it won't make him truthful.

LOT OF BOTTLE

TWO SEA ANGLERS are celebrating hooking a 17th-century wine bottle which could be worth thousands of pounds. Stephen Gosling, of London, and Ralph Willoughby, of Bexley, were fishing near Herne Bay, in the Thames estuary, when they had their historic catch. "We took it to Rochester museum who dated the bottle to between 1690 and 1710," said Stephen, 41. There has been wild speculation about its value, with some claims as high as £10,000. Steve added: "We're just savouring the moment as it's a nice bit of history."

AN ANGLERS FAST FOOD RESTAURANT

HAPPY HOOKERS

TWENTY-FIVE barking-mad Brummies caused more than a stir on the bank when they turned up for a match dressed as hookers. It was away with the Halkon-Hunt fishing gear and on with the see-through blouses, short skirts, stockings and suspenders for the event on the River Huntspill at Withy Grove. But it was all for a good cause – the lad(ie)s from the Nachelles Park AC raised well over £1,000 for the Birmingham Children's Hospital with their antics. "It was quite worrying really because everyone couldn't wait to get dressed up," said organiser Seamus Bourke. "They all insisted it was the first time they had done this sort of thing but some of them carried it off just too convincingly for my liking!"

FISHERMAN'S FRIENDS

You know that you are a real fisherman when all of your wife's Christmas presents come from the tackle store!

IN THE SWIM

STUNNED ANGLER Paul Clarke nearly drowned when a car rolled down a hill and catapulted him into a lake. Paul was talking tactics at Hallcroft Fishery, Notts, when, unknown to him, a Citroen Xantia sped towards him after its handbrake apparently failed. He turned round just in time to be sent flying into the water. Non-swimmer Paul was left gripping on to the car until two friends dived in to save him.

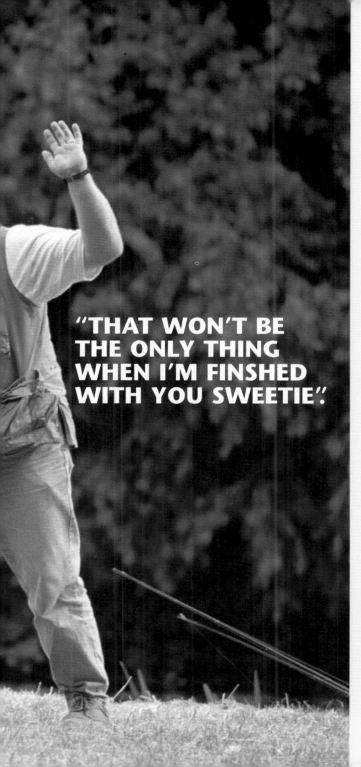

"THAT WON'T BE THE ONLY THING WHEN I'M FINSHED WITH YOU SWEETIE".

THAT'S NO BONEFISH

A BRITISH ANGLER was dragged six miles into the Pacific Ocean after hooking a world-record giant trevally (a member of the jack family). Intrepid Stephen Collis bent into the 75lb 8oz monster during a big-game fishing holiday. "I didn't think it was ever going to end," said Stephen. "I even considered cutting the line to escape." Stephen was casting a fly for bonefish over coral flats on big fish Mecca Christmas Island when he saw the trevally gliding in front of him – then its gaping mouth engulfed his yellow bucktail fly. "There was an 80 foot drop at the end of the coral so I jumped into a friend's rubber dinghy and the fish towed me further and further out to sea." After a two-hour struggle using just a 20lb line, Stephen got the fish ashore.

FISH & QUIPS

Why don't sharks attack lawyers?
Professional courtesy.

87

ALL PEGGED OUT

GEOFF DODSWORTH was pleased to draw peg 45 during a match on the Sawmills stretch of the River Nidd, at Knaresborough. That is, until he saw what was floating in front of him. "I've seen clothing in the river before, but I could also see a head and shoulders," said a shocked Geoff. "We all agreed it was real and called the police." A spokesman for Harrogate Police said: "We thought it may have been a kids' prank with a bonfire night guy. It turned out to be a man who had been missing since November 5, which is ironic, really."

RAINING MAGGOTS

AN ANGLER sprayed maggots over diners on a canal barge in a rare case of rod rage. The fed-up fisher saw red when his swim was ruined by passing boat traffic. So he took aim and fired his maggots on to boat users as they tucked into their meal, forcing them to baton down the hatches and beat a hasty retreat.

ANGLERS - THEY'RE MAD!!

HE COMES
FROM
EALING

FIRST THINGS FIRST

A NEVER-SAY-DIE specimen hunter landed a huge bream minutes after breaking his leg. Simon Pharoah shattered his leg bone and passed out after slipping on the wet bank as he battled the Tyson-like slab. When he came round, he noticed the fish was still hooked so he fought through the pain barrier to net the mighty eight pounder. Simon, who might not be able to walk again for 15 weeks, insists it was all worthwhile. He said: "Fish are more important than my leg. I'm just disappointed I didn't get a photo."

AVON FAREWELL

LIFELONG ANGLER Albert Lea had his ashes scattered on his favourite peg on the Warwickshire Avon. Albert's widow, Doreen, granted Albert his final wish during an emotional ceremony on the banks of his beloved river. His family also placed flowers on the spot where Albert, who died aged 63, spent hundreds of happy hours hauling in chub and barbel. Son-in-law Terry Simcox said: "He had fished from that peg for 14 years. Thank the Lord he got his first day's fishing of the season in before he died."

"IF SANTA DIDN'T SPEND SO MUCH TIME FISHING MY SON BEN WOULD HAVE GOT HIS TELE-TUBBY FOR CHRISTMAS"

SANTA SPENT MUCH OF JANUARY CLEARING UP ALL THE DROPPINGS FROM HIS REINDEERS. SOME ARE HARDER TO REACH THAN OTHERS

DO THEY THINK I'M
THAT STUPID TO FALL
FOR THAT BAIT - IT DOES
LOOK QUITE TASTY
THOUGH.

A PROFESSIONAL ANGLER DEEP IN TRAINING

BASS FRAUD SURFACES

A WORLD RECORD fish caught in the USA more than 40 years ago has been exposed as a fraud. Tennessee angler David L Hayes captured an 11lb 15oz smallmouth bass from Kentucky's Dale Hollow Lake in 1955. The specimen set a new international Game Fish Association All-Tackle record but now David's guide at the time has admitted stuffing the fish with lead weights. David was unaware of John Barlow's ploy, which the guide said he did to boost his business. Six weeks after the catch, John's conscience got the better of him and he had a sworn affidavit drawn up. He sent the document to the US Army Corps of Engineers, who managed the lake at the time, but they wrote back saying the matter was nothing to do with them. It appears John forgot the incident, until Army staff uncovered the document just weeks ago! IGFA President, Mike Leech, said: "It certainly is the strangest story I've heard in all my years of fishing. Obviously his conscience got the better of him and he couldn't keep the secret any longer!"

The world record has now been awarded to Kentucky angler John Gorman, who landed a 10lb 14oz smallmouth from the same venue in 1969.

MATCHLESS MISERY

UNLUCKY Dave Jacques thought he was on to a flyer when he reeled in a perch just 10 seconds after casting out on Walsall's Rushall Canal. But a catalogue of disasters kicked off when first Dave's pole was run over by a towpath cyclist, then a stray dog cocked its leg on his jacket. Just when he thought nothing else could go wrong, one of his bait tubs was knocked over by a playful Alsatian, leaving Dave to sit out the rest of the match fishless. Luckless Dave added: "We all went to the pub afterwards, and after a day like that I needed a drink." But, much to his pals' amusement, Dave dipped out again when the barmaid told him his favourite beer was off.

**TINA TURNER'S
CAREER HAD
TAKEN A NOSE
DIVE.**

SOMETHING FISHY IN THE AIR

A WOMAN has been attacked by a shoal of dead fish as she unpacked her weekly shopping. Ruth Harnett heard a thud on her car roof as she reached into the boot of her car. When she turned to investigate, she noticed 20 dead roach lying around. Ruth, 27, of Hatfield, Herts, said: "The fish were between two and five inches long and were dead when they landed. I picked them up and put them in my freezer." Oddly enough, a similar thing happened to her grandfather many years ago in Welwyn Garden City – just seven miles away as the fish flies. A spokesman for the Met Office explained that pockets of warm air can rise, picking up things from the water and dropping them on land.

PHILOSOFISHY

Nothing increases the size of your catch as much as the absence of witnesses!

99

A NICE AU PAIR THERE

Hammersmith, London

I AM WRITING this letter on behalf of our Polish au pair, Tonia Zwalak. She has read Des Taylor's article on women and fishing, with which she disagrees. As she can read English better than she can write it, she has asked me to write this letter for her. I reproduce her words verbatim:

'I am mad with Des Taylor's talking on women and fishy. I am 18 years of old and am handling many big Poles in my country, when I am angling on the Bug (I believe the Bug is a river near her home). The family (that's us, incidentally) take me fishy to carps lake and I catch many carps. The men were showing me how to catch them, and handle their tackle also. As very hot, many of men stop to watch me. Des Taylor is wrong saying women and fish not mix-up, the men like me, and are giving me phone numbers to ring up for fish business.'

There you have it. It seems that women anglers are more appreciated in Britain than Des thinks.

Ian D. Burton, on behalf of Tonia

FISH & QUIPS

You know you are a real fisherman when you go fishing on your Wedding Day.

FISH & QUIPS

You know you are a real fisherman when your bait bills exceed your grocery bills.

PHILOSOFISHY

Do you think fish brag about the size of the man he got away from?

ANGLING, A
SPORT FOR
GENTLEMEN,
LADIES, AND
EVERYTHING
INBETWEEN.

MAN'S BEST FRIEND?

I AIN'T COMING
ANYWHERE NEAR
YOU... 6 HOURS ON
A RIVERBANK,
GROPING FISH...
I'M SORRY BUT YOU
STINK!

HE'S BEHIND YOU!

ANGLING TIMES reader Dave Munroe, 31, recalled how he was pulling dace and roach from his local River Mole when he heard a munching noise behind him. Turning round he discovered a horse tucking into his umbrella.

"He then started to eat my rod bag so I decided to move to another peg – but he just followed me," said Dave, of West Molesey. The hungry horse then cornered Dave before the Surrey rod – fully laden with all his equipment on his back – tried to escape. "I was making it across the field when it head-butted me in the back and sent me flying. Then a man out walking his dog saw what was happening and legged it as well. Imagine the scene, two men and a dog being seen off by a big cart horse! At the time it frightened the life out of me but now I find it hilarious and so do my mates – they keep coming up behind me shouting 'neigh'!"

LOST YOUR CHOPPERS?

A MYSTERY angler may be having trouble at meal times... after leaving his false teeth at his peg! The rogue set of gnashers was found at Billingham Lake, near Rye, Kent, by Clive Vale Angling Club member Ron Hodd. If you are one of the 600-strong Clive Vale AC with teething troubles, Ron's yer man.

WHAT ABOUT ANGLING?

BBC CHIEFS once again snubbed angling at last year's Sports Personality of the Year award. Fishing had enjoyed a golden summer which produced two English world champions – in contrast to other sports. Barnsley ace Alan Scotthorne, 35, who was ignored after first winning the World Championship, blasted: "It's disgusting. It would be nice to mix with the stars and represent the sport but I think tiddly winks comes above angling. It's supposed to be one of the most popular participation sports so there should be some sort of recognition from the BBC."

NO SPIKE NOT TONIGHT I'VE GOT A HEADACHE.

MY HOW SANTA'S ELVES HAVE GROWN

SANTA WAS REDUCED TO DESPERATE MEASURES TO FULFIL THIS CHRISTMAS'S PRESENT QUOTA.

HARRY'S A GROUPIE

ONE MAN has been on the bank with the England team more times than champions Bob Nudd and Alan Scotthorne put together. For 83-year-old Brummie Harry Tatton is the country's most loyal supporter. He's followed the lads at every World Championship and Home International since Dave Thomas took the world crown on the River Avon in 1981. "I haven't got a favourite angler because they're all good," says Harry. "But I was very lucky to sit behind Kim Milsom when he won a bronze medal. It was really fantastic."

ILLEGAL SPECIES

THE ENVIRONMENT AGENCY admits it is powerless to stop the tidal wave of illegal fish flooding into Britain. EA spokesman Brendan Paddy conceded: "Even if it's completely obvious someone has illegally introduced fish, there's very little we can do."

WORDS OF WISDOM

AN UNHOLY ROW broke out when a fishing match was targeted by Jehovah's Witnesses. A determined preacher moved from peg to peg looking for converts and handing out copies of the evangelical magazine, *Watchtower*. But his sermon was cut short when fed-up fisherman Derek Hassle barked a few short, sharp words of wisdom of his own – along the lines of 'go forth and multiply'. Sadly Derek of Warrington, Cheshire, went on to finish in last place with a dry net.

WHAT A PAIR OF TITS

THE ARSE END
OF FISHING.

GRIM DOUBLE

A TOP matchman has been nicknamed 'the Undertaker' after finding dead bodies in his swim on two consecutive fishing trips. Andy Gregory made the first of his grim discoveries during an Acton AC Open match on the Grand Union Canal at Camley Street.

The 32-year-old West Londoner said: "I was catching steadily and well on my way to victory when the police turned up and told everyone to go home. Being on winning form there was no way I was until a dead body came floating past! It was a bit shocking – and I only managed fourth place in the end." Less than two weeks later, and just five miles up the road at the GUC's Hole-in-the-Wall stretch, Andy made his second shocking find. "Something suddenly bobbed into my swim. I prodded it with my pole and it turned out to be a badly decomposed body." After calling the police, Andy left quickly, fearing being linked to a double murder.

IF ALL ELSE FAILS

TAKE THE LEAVES and fruit of the spurge (Euphorbia), throw both in a fish pond or in other water where many fishes are, which fishes eat of this herb or weed and become so drunk by it that they turn their belly up as if they were dead, only they come back to themselves and that does not injure them. Then throw them in fresh water, and they recover; thus they are taken with the hands.

Dit Boecxken, Antwerp, circa 1492

LILY-LIVERED CHUB

THEY [chub] are cowardly, inasmuch that if you once turn them, they are presently dispirited and you manage them as you please. For this reason some waggish, merry Anglers compare them to Portuguese Soldiers, who have very little inclination to fighting at any time, even tho' the defence of their Country requires them, and if their enemy make a vigorous attack, they immediately turn tail, and it is twenty to one if you can prevail with them, by any means to face about.

From The Gentleman Angler, *1726*

IF YOU ENJOYED THIS BOOK, WHAT ABOUT THESE!

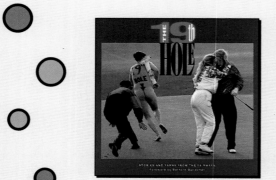

All these books are available at your local book shop or can be ordered direct from the publisher. Just list the titles you require and give your name address, including postcode.

Prices and availability are subject to change without notice.

Please send to Chameleon Cash Sales, 76 Dean Street, London W1V 5HA, a cheque or postal order for £7.99 and add the following for postage and packaging:

UK - £1.00 For the first book, 50p for the second and 30p for the third and for each additional book up to a maximum of £3.00.

OVERSEAS - (including Eire) £2.00 For the first book, £1.00 for the second and 50p for each additional book up to a maximum of £3.00.